AF485835

This is for the great Lorna Pinkney and my family at Tuesday Verses. Thank all of you for being so warm, welcoming and loving. I am always grateful for your hospitality and for giving people a space to help us grow our creativity.

Versatile

(verse-a-tile)

A collection of poems, verses
and illustrations
by Ashton Lee

Table of Contents

Table of Contents

BOOK I

Only God can judge
But the rest of the world is
The prosecution

Complex

Me and God been estranged
But I still call him
Mainly to say thanks for lookin' out
Life could've went some different routes
But I save hypotheticals
For my scripts
Giving tour guides of my mind
Through different lips

Wish Dad was here to see this
But I want Ma to see it more
Worked her ass off
So I can pay dues and settle scores
Divorce kid
Learned to take bumps early
My struggle wasn't unique
But it don't make me less worthy

Great is thy faithfulness
Always seeing mercy
Though karma might sneak up
For the times I moved dirty
That's when I was in the church
Demons been surrounded me
Passed down by family
Adapted to environments

Fed by the media
See the hell fire lit
Debaucherous to calm the fuss
Of butterflies in the pit
Of my stomach
Might confess it in a booth
Then show I'm living proof
That it's best to live your truth

The Experience

Being a horny virgin
Is like being hooked on a drug
That you've never tried
Everyone knows what that's like
It might've been a minute for some
But we all know
We knew what it was
Before we even knew what it was

Childhood games like
"Show me yours and I'll show you mine"
Revealed the road to our destiny
A day that we look forward to
Like a baby taking their first step
It's the peak of maturity
And the climax to many a story

Those who've done it
Might say it's no big deal
But they know the feeling
Of loins aching with frustration
Only knowing thirst
While being surrounded by moisture
Hoping their tongues
Can one day get a taste
Or at least touch the tip

Parents and churches
Call it purity
Like virgins are babies
Who should be shielded
From sexual desire
Little do they know
If cushions and teddy bears could talk
The stories they would tell

We all know what it is
Just like we all know the risks
And people still DARE
To throw caution into the wind
And make that jump
Without a parachute, no less
No matter how many bumps they get
No matter how many people get bruised

They'll even ignore death
Just to feel that high
So to be a person
Who has never had sex
Seeing what it does to others
Only for them to come back for more
That must be some good shit

Sex may not be everything
But not having it sure is
Does that mean people should be
Pressured into a habit?
Of course not
But at the end of the day
We're all just a bunch of crack babies
Hoping to get a hit

Thank You

I want to say thank you
to those who still cry out
in a world designed to break souls

Thank you for
not letting waves of bad news
drown your expressions

Helplessness is the new normal
it's not hard to go numb
so easy toss away shock
as being taboo

Evil has a way of hollowing you out
until all you are is just surface

So from the bottom of my heart
thank you for
finding a way to still feel

Expensive

Sallie Mae changed her name
But it's still the same damage
After bills, I ask myself
How I'm s'posed to manage
My job answers that question
Every two weeks
That's the next check
Lather, rinse and repeat

I hate the hard labor
But must hide the expressions
Stock in the company
I need to check investments
I live outside of work
But I must follow my lessons:
Try to save, cover your ass
And use protection

Because being alive
Is expensive
Just to get by
Most have to be inventive
Turning into engineers
So they can survive
If given that opportunity
So many would thrive

Can't imagine
Being a full parent
With aspirations, so my freedom
I do cherish
But peace to them
For wearing that belt
Fighting the cycle so their kids
Can know wealth

Expensive cont.

Or at least
See decent Christmases
So thank God for second jobs
And side businesses
God bless
Those who even take classes
Working towards degrees
While still having mouths to feed

And that's with no shade
If you hustle from day to day
Putting yourself aside
To give your kids a better way
My mom raised two by herself
So I see it
Praying I have even half that strength
If I be it

BOOK
II

The switch of her hips
When she walks works like a watch
Swaying back and forth

Dreams (Homage to Biggie)

I have dreams of dating a singer
I could get with a SZA
Have Janelle Monae want to spend the day
And make Ri-Ri see she neeeeeeed me
I may seem average to you
But my love jones chill bones
Like ice cream cones
If my words don't get her
She'll be hooked off my Tony. Toni. Tone!

If her voice can glide
I need her by my side
Sharing my world
With my Mary J. Blige
I won't just be
An accessory
Al B. Sure
To give the best of me

I'll inspire her next song
As she hums along
To the sound of my heartbeat
The words form through our feet
As we perform poetry in motion
Vowing to give
A lifetime of devotion

Our love will be the masterpiece
Her greatest release
All's fair in love and war
But I'll be her peace
I'll be Luther to her Cheryl
The Pip to her Gladys
Hitting all the right notes
Backing her up cause she's the baddest

Dreams cont.

Crying no more like Ms. Tina
We'll be like Christina
Running through peaks and valleys
Without feeling stripped
Her song will be of joy
Happy to breathe again
Cause she switched from being with Boys
To being with Men

Delucious (de-lust-cious)

She can be drawn to money
And the way her lover looks
But nothing's sexier to a woman
Than when you cook
She'll appreciate jewelry
And brand names for her feet
But an underrated fact
Is that women love to eat

Dope boys ain't the only ones
Who whip it in the kitchen
What you know about ten different ways
To cook chicken?
Baked, fried and grilled
With sweet potatoes and spinach
Ice cream on a freshly baked brownie
As the finish

You can satisfy em all
From picky eaters to foodies
That itis puts em to sleep
While these goofys need roofies
But who needs force
She won't resist your dishes
If you add some olive oil
She'll want to be your Mrs.

Let her tongue savor the flavor
Once it passes her lips
Bet her eyes'll roll back
When it touches the tip
Different recipies on deck
Choose your own adventure
Experiment with ingredients
Give her something to remember

Delucious cont.

The smell alone
Brings a tingling sensation
Serving steaks thick and juicy
Just say she's the inspiration
All that passion she'll be tastin'
Will make signals hit her brain
That'll make her speak in tongues
Ecstasy escapes her lungs

Give it to her how she likes it
You best know how to handle her
If practice makes perfection
Then stamina's not a challenger
Breakfast, lunch and dinner
You can last all day
Apply your skills to seafood
It's basically foreplay

You can master the language of love
In culinary arts
But nothing's cunning when you're lingual
If you speak from the heart
If you take your time
To make sure it's done right
Food poisoning won't be
What leaves y'all hot and sweaty tonight

Animal can be specialty
But don't limit
Vegetarians can get it
With broccoli patties and biscuits
She'll cheat on Ramadan
For some eggplant parmesan
Tweak it for the vegans
Y'all won't even need garments on

Worth It

Forever
Is a ways away
But it feels so nice to have my lady
Be part of my day to day
It's only the beginning
But I think it's safe to say
I've never felt this way before
So I really wanna pour

My all in this
Moving faster than what I'm used to
But I guess it's different
When you're dealing with a mutual
Both of us taking time
To work on ourselves
Breaking out of our shells
So we won't have to dwell

Stripping off layers
From a lifetime of hell
So if this leads to birth
There's a Heaven on Earth
We're not there yet
It's still the honeymoon phase
We've yet to show our real selves
In our darker days

The bad habits and ways
Through time they can illuminate
But thank God we're practicing patience
And to communicate
We know that this
Won't be all cinnamon
This love shit is work
But if they're worth it, get it in

A Bootyful Poem

The butt is the part of the body
That's one of the best-est
Not only should it be loved
It should be respected
Sir Mix-a-Lot
Introduced us to this precious
Most beautifullest thing
It's almost angelic

And if it has a cushion
You can't help but behold it some
It keeps eyes glued
Even if it ain't in motion
And when it is
The jiggle of the cheeks
Are like waves to an ocean
Inspiring thoughts

That are best kept disclosed in
The back of the mind
That parallels other's
Whenever they see a fine
Dime on the dance floor
Back it up and wine
Folks on the sideline
Tryin to grow a spine

To walk up and ask
For a little bump and grind
Probably couldn't handle shawty
Throwing that behind
Showing off what they learned
On the internet and tv
Practiced in the mirror
To make it look easy

18

It's so interestin'
All the various
Definitions and shapes
And the reactions that you get from them
Many get it
From mama's good eatin
But what's in that cornbread
That they be feedin em?

Let's start with
What many would call "long backs"
If you love yourself
There's not a thing wrong with that
You're still beautiful
Never forget
So if someone talks shit
Just say "I can still sit"

But then there's the raindrop
It's small but that's fine
Some do squats
To make it look divine
Even if you don't exercise
It don't matter
You know if you wear those good jeans
There's nobody badder

Then there's "The Beyonce"
Which the size of the butt
Is based, on the wideness of the hips
To the waist
The cushion all around
Gives your bottom help
Showing it from the front
It can't hide itself

A Bootyful Poem cont.

Then there's the onion
Pokin' out that round shape
That thang lookin' healthy
An orbit you can't escape
You can be super thick
Or skinny as toothpicks
You walk by, even your enemies
Be like "Ooh shit"

Some might get annoyed
When it's treated like a fetish
But it's so powerful
You can use it as leverage
You don't need the whole world
Giving it inspections
But I bet you smile
Seeing it in your reflection

BOOK

III

My anxiety
Completes me like a lover
I was born married

Filter

In a world that disregards God
It's hard not to be on guard
Spirits slippin'
To superficial religions
For props people paint their lives
As unbelievable
Open books praying we skim
Instead of reading you

So glad I didn't have Instagram
As a youth
Pictures speak 1000 words
Doesn't mean it tells the truth
Captions and filters
That can brighten every tooth
In your grin, but step outside
And show the dark within

Spilling guts on Facebook
and Twitter
Talking trash but post a pic
To show that ain't nobody lit-ter
Getting all the likes
When you pump the positivity
I'd be scrolling wishing
I had the same energy

Turning myself
Into my worst enemy
Magazines are dead
This covers a wider spread
Every day folks faking
Like their lives can't be attainable
So when you're feeling low
It looks like happiness ain't for you

A Child's Place

I'm an energetic child
So they say I need pills
I can never put my dreams
In their proper place
So this is supposed to organize me
Pop one
And it floats down to my system
Like a cunning mercenary
To put my brain in a sleeper hold

Now I can be the nice little statue
My teacher wants me to be
Because every lesson plan for them
Is to get through the day
And that requires silence
To be so quiet
That you can hear my spit drop
No roaming
No "pspspspsps"
No questions
Not pre-approved by the board

All of my pencil movements
Are now in a controlled manner
This is how it should be
I'd probably do better
With a more suitable teacher
Or a different class
But to most adults a child's place
Is in line

Soon I become the model student
An example for the rest
To be subdued enough to submit
To be present enough to pass
On to the next grade

Rageaholic

Check the
Blood content
It's high enough to be unconscious
Conscience
And common sense are lost
When intoxicated
Tumbling down the wrong path
When the fade hits

Red faced
When you're on that dark
The sick from inside
You start to barf
And get it on other people
And reactions spark
A whole domino effect
Which drives you to a wreck

This will never take the edge off
You know that
Still you ignore the pleas
To control that
In this cold world
The heat will help you fend
Til you don't know where the trouble starts
And the habit ends

Take a microscope
And look at your DNA
See how your parents were
Fucked up back in the day
Throwing shots
To make their targets feel useless
Showing that you don't need to do rounds
To be abusive

Rageaholic cont.

You swore up and down
You wouldn't be like them
Til you see reality
Can be quite grim
And it's worse when they see
That you share those traits
Your parents punishing you
Because you relate

Adding to your fate
You can barely control the impulse
Where anything can drag you in
Even the smallest insult
To popping off the bottle
Going hardcore
Drowning in the haze
Til you're passed out on the floor

The Prison

I feel like a prisoner
Secluded in my own head
I get so caught up and lost in my thoughts
That I can't view
What's happening in the world around me
Even conversations
Are stunted by a glass divider
I try to break myself out
But I end up getting caught
And drug back in
At times it can serve as a sanctuary
But mostly it's a dark cage
Where the functions of my cell stare at me
With varied convictions

The walls of dead memories
Echo screams of judgement
From a childhood, eons ago
Yet the voices sound as crisp
As if my bullies and family
Were right in front of me
Reminding me that I'm not "normal"
They looked down on me
Just like my ceiling coated with fears
Anxiety peering over me
Like God adding up my sins
I worry that the weight of failure
Will cause the ceiling to collapse on me
Breaking every bone in my body
Leaving me to suffocate and die

The gravity of it all pulls me
Into the floor of regret
I'm haunted by the ghost
Of shoulda, woulda, coulda

The Prison cont.

The times I should've stood up for myself
The wish that I wasn't so awkward
The people whom I've hurt
By being my messy, irritated self
I lie helplessly
Marinated in gloom
The metal bars look like teeth
Chewing at my soul
I see what life has done to me
Through the shine in their reflection
What was once a solid form
Is now a disfigured blob

I call my mind a prison
Because it's something I can't escape
While I can do wonders with it
It's also the main thing
That holds me back
It's been my gift and my curse
Ever since I was born
But even in captivity
I learn to appreciate its gift

I take it like a ray of morning sunshine
Beaming goodness
Through that small window of hope
And I make sure I stand under it
Allowing it to dry me of the gloom
As I absorb its vitamin C
Because as much as I hate being trapped here
It's my home
It can either break me
Or I can make the best of it
I just need to work on
How to do the latter

30

BOOK IV

I miss trapping my
Fingers into your tangles
This can't be freedom

Like A Drug

The High...
Your love is like a drug
You've gotten under my skin
And no matter what I do
I can't escape you
But why would I want to?
The first taste of you
Was like I was being
Hugged by Heaven
My heart races
From your scent
And I melt like putty
From your touch
Time doesn't exist
When we lay together
Doing nothing
But sharing each other's energy
Your presence is nourishment
To my soul
It's more than just a trance
I want to eat, sleep and breathe you

The Haze...
Your love is like a drug
I often wonder
If you mean to leave bruises
But I remind myself
That's part of the rush
Whether blow or brush
I'm just thankful for you touch
Love is pain
And you hurt so good
Just ignore my wince
Ignore my will
Ignore my humanity

Like A Drug cont.

Just know that my soul is yours
What is my job
Except to serve you?
What is time with my family
Except a distraction from you
My only altar
Is the ground you walk on
Throw me to hell
And I'll crawl back to you on my knees
Because I live for your rush
Blow or brush

The Crash...

Your love is like a drug
I lay in fetal position
Everything feels numb
Except for my pounding head
My face pulled down by gravity
My heart withered and blackened
Like a dead plant
My soul drained from my body
Just like my money
My friends and family
Warned me about you
Now they see me
And barely recognize me
The tears that they fight
When they see my toothless smile
All of the good feelings I had
Is not worth the hell I'm in
I know that now
I don't know how to escape
But I know that I have to
Because your love is like a drug
And it will be the death of me

36

Store RUN!!!

Sweatpants cover
Undeoterized flesh
Tight tank top
Barely containing her chest
She walks into the drug store
Feeling like a mess
Caught the eye of a thirsty brother
Adding to her stress

Ol' boy didn't want to just
Stop at the stare
He just had to talk to her
Followed her everywhere
Her replies to him
Were short and simple
Cause she just wants some medicine
The girl has the sniffles

She wants to pay the cashier
He wants to be her boyfriend
Wouldn't stop so her last resort
To his annoyin'
Ass was catch an attitude
It's bad to do that to a dude
Cause hurting his pride
Leads to irrational

Reactions now he's snappin'
Because she clowned him
Went out to the parking lot
Ignoring his surroundings
He yells out "Bitch!"
Now he's went too far
So she turns around to see him...
Get hit by a car

Another You (Homage to Beyoncé)

Do you really think
I care about finding another you?
You must not know how a breakup works
Here's the premise:
Your participation in my life
Makes me unhappy
So for me to be happy again
You must leave my life
I don't care where you go
I don't care who you end up with
As long as you're away from me

Being with you
Was like watching a terrible movie
I went in thinking that
I would enjoy myself
Ten minutes in
Everything went downhill
The main character was unlikable
The dialogue was shallow
And it went on for far too long
So if I didn't like the first one
Why would I want a sequel?

What I want is someone
Who doesn't burn bridges
Like it's their career
Someone who doesn't treat
Different opinions like threats
I tried to find love
In your dark suffocating abyss
Instead I absorbed your energy
Where everything I touched
Got close to withering

And while you're fine to live in suffering
I'll no longer make space
And lose anyone else
Like I lost myself with you

Now there may be a chance
You were also unhappy
While we were together
But I'd argue that misery is your default
And the type of help that you need
Is a squad made of Jesus,
Buddha, Gandhi, Dr. King
And Seigmond Frued
Armed with marijuana
And tranquilizer darts
To both calm you down
And fix the festering cyst
That you call a heart

I sincerely pray you get that help
In fact I pray that
You are relieved of all your demons
That one day you will embrace love
And make amends
With everyone that you've hurt
But even if you did all of that
Don't you ever think for a second
That even then I'd want you back
And here you are thinking
That I'll be pressed
To find another person like you

Shhiiiiiieeeeet

How Much

How much will it cost
To tell me that you're all mine?
To make me believe that my charm
Was the key to your heart
That no one else gives you
The feeling that I give you

How much will it cost
To make every kiss feel inspired?
Like it's me you crave
Don't make it vague
Tell me I'm your number one
Though I probably
Don't even crack your top ten

Lie to me please
Everyone knows
How much the truth hurts
I've experienced enough truths
So your lies
Will be a breath of fresh air

I just want my gullibility to run wild
Someone to fool me
Into believing they're a fool for me
Just for a little while
There's no attachments
Just me emptying my pockets
In exchange for pure bliss

I'm sure you can relate a little
Too many of us learn the hard way
To never to award ourselves

To someone for nothing
At least here, there's a payoff
We scratch each other's itches
Til we both leave relieved

So please, lie to me
Give me your Oscar winning performance
Touch me like I'm worthy
Look at me like I'm someone
Make my needs
Stop feeling like fantasies
Make me feel handsome
And I'll pay you handsomely

BOOK
V

I call us Da GAWD
Because we're all creators
And we deserve praise

Mediums

I wish my destruction was cool enough
To put in a song
Where my demons float on a melody
That breezes through your ears
The beauty cuts so deep
Your tears flow like an opened vein
I'd lay down my wounds
For you to tap your feet
Or be intimate with your partner
Trying to make your moans of pleasure
Match my moans of angst

Instead I'm just regular ol' boring destructive
Angst is the lonely corner that I sit in
As I binge on my wounds in silence
Wiping my mouth on paper
And tossing it anywhere
I say that I'll pick it up eventually
But the trash piles up
Almost like I'm saving it
Almost like if I keep it long enough
It can be useful again

Never Leave That Out

Art is a high
I keep chasing so it never dies
While Imposter Syndrome
Tells me lies
Like I'm not flying
Cause I don't aim for the sky
Forgetting all the times
I floated on cloud 9

I know I pay too much attention
To end results
Of other people
And that's my fault
Just because a story ended
Doesn't mean your life's complete
With every level we reach
A new challenge to beat

Hell, I look up to legends
Who still gotta eat
Pray I never forget em
No matter the size of seat
I sit at any table
If I'm able, show I'm grateful
Even at my lowest now
I give to those less stable

Cause I know what it's like
To struggle to live
Life to it's fullest
Biting so many bullets
To reach that point of happiness
People dream about
You've worked hard to make it so far
Never leave that out

My Worst Enemy

I've been bullied by peers
Mistreated by family
Played by friends
And wounded by lovers
But none of them can hold a candle
To my absolute worst enemy: Me

I don't know what I ever did to me
But I got BEEF
And always on sight
I can't pass a mirror
Without hearing slander
Since the bullies from school
Ain't here no more
My reflection takes their place
"fat..." "ugly..." "dumb..."
Hell, I don't even need words
Just a dirty look and scoff

If words don't work, it gets physical
I'm quick to get in my way
When I start making moves
If I maneuver around
Then I trip myself up
And don't let me move with a strut
Cause then I'm followed by a creep
Armed with a jagged memory
Sneaking to get up close then BAM!
Knocked to the ground
My head pounding
As I hear laughter and taunts
"I know you ain't tryna feel good
Must've forgot all your failures, huh?"

My Worst Enemy cont.

Now I could be the bigger person
Reach out with a helping hand
Because hurt people, hurt people
And love heals all wounds
I could...
I really could...
But the way my grudge is set up
I don't play that shit
I don't know who I think I am
Just know it ain't the one

But see, I used to strike fear in me
Because I weaponized my anxiety
But as years passed it got dull
And I sharpened
Built confidence and grew strength
Learned to endure pressure
By stepping back
Clearing my mind
And taking breaths
That way when it's time to strike back
I do it with force

So now when I pass by my mirror
And my reflection talks shit
I say "You know damn well I'm pretty"
And keep it moving
If I get in my way, I throw bows
If I try to trip, I kick shins
And as for that jagged memory
That was just a hard lesson
It used to break me
Now I break it
And leave my foe stunned

48

With all the victories
I know there'll be more attempts
More remarks, more blocks,
More rough thoughts
But my fights with peers and loved ones
Trained me for this
So when the time comes
And it's on once again
Imma kick my ass
And Imma keep kickin my ass
Until I learn to put some respect on my name

Verses

At times it can feel worthless
To just lay down verses
But at least there are people
Who encourage us hard workers
If you're the type to curse us
That just means you don't deserve us
And proving haters wrong
Can make it all worth it

Cause those who want to make a mark
Start off by swimming with sharks
Who try to rip them apart
So there'll be scars
And maybe even limbs missin'
It's God's tradition
Though the heat's unbearable
We stay in the kitchen

Before the book
Our lives were purpose driven
And when we speak up some folks
Might cover up so they won't listen
But we stay on our mission
There's no way to deny us
We can move a crowd
To start riots

And shut down any oppressive system
Like a virus
We let out our aggression
With this form of expression
Just to let you know
That you're lucky it ain't physical
We're not all brawlers
But we're sick of being seen as pitiful

As personal as we take it
How can we fake it
We're trying to save our souls
Not just make a statement
That's how some of us
Became somebody's favorite
Cause we spoke to a moment
Where they felt they couldn't make it

So for you, it's entertainment
But for us this is sacred
We learn to "Live Love"
If we feel it we create it
For you, it's entertainment
But for us this is sacred
Long Live Lorna
If we feel it we create it

Verses

Thank Yous and Shout-Outs

God-Thank You for sparing my messy, complicated self throughout the years. I'm slowly realizing how to make it all work. Much love.

Ma-I owe so much to you. Thank you for being my biggest supporter. I'm proud of you and I love you very much.

My brother, LaJuan-I'm proud of who you've become and I know that you will grow to be even greater. Thank you for always being open to hear me and for being honest. I love you.

My girlfriend, Cherrell-I live for your smile. I'm all ears for your insight. I will forever root for your success. I love you so much and I'm glad to have you in my life.

Charles-Big bro! I'm always thinking of you. I hope all of your days are blessed. I love you.

Ajtiim-Thank you for always giving a motivational word and going the extra mile for those you love. I love you, big bro.

Beverly-I love you sis. We're gonna party together again soon. Til then, God bless.

Roscoe Burnems-From coaching to inspiring, you made me step my writing up. I'm forever grateful. Keep holding it down for Richmond.

My good friends, Kashif & Jernelle-Thank you both for being warm and welcoming and for giving

52

Thank Yous and Shout-Outs cont.

me the space to be less guarded. Your passions and good spirits will pay off in a big way, I know it.

My mentor, Vickie Scallion-I wouldn't be who I was if it wasn't for you and HATTheatre. You have truly saved my life and I'm forever grateful. I love you.

To my family at Tuesday Verses- Bitew, Gady and the hard working staff at Addis Ethiopian Restaurant, Jamila Williams, Nickey McMullen, Paula G. Akinwole, Dee Gee, Mikki Robinson, Eric Dugan, Shon Davis, Radio B, Nadira Chase, Marcus EShadd, Jess Snyder, Micah "Bam-Bamm" White, Onajé Baldwin, The Few, Tracey Brown, Zbey Tha-Poet, B Lovee, Nikka Sharee, Lee "Narrator" Jones, Samia Minnicks, Ajani Sekou, Versastyles, Michelle Dodd, The Stuttering Poet, Breeze The Poet, Megan Rickman Blackwood, The 2 Up 2 Down Band, and a special shout out to Wednesday Night Verses. To anyone who I forgot, I apologize; thank you all for being so instrumental to such a loving and open experience.

And most importantly, thank you Lorna Pinckney for giving so many artists a home and a place to feel loved. And most of all for being your lovely beautiful self. Rest In Power.

Additional shout-outs-Maria & Darmon Smalls, Uncle Norbert, Marian Fields, Uncle Lestor, Uncle Carrol and Auntie Faye, Shanna & Alvin Mosby, Quinton Taylor, Marcus Henderson... **cont.**

Thank Yous and Shout-Outs cont.

the Branch family, the Sommerville family, ALL of my cousins (Lee, Fields and Clarke), ALL of my nieces & nephews, my HATTheatre family, St. James Baptist Church, King Davis, Carolyn Davis, VCU's own Students United, Kr3ative M1ndz, the homies Jay Guevara and Rieka Speaks and my fam at The Writer's Den

Rest in Power to all of my loved ones who returned to the essence. Thank you for your time here. Please watch over us and keep us proteted.

Ashton Lee is a multi-layered artist who doesn't play about his craft. In 2009 he received his bachelor's degree in graphic design from Marymount University. Since 2011, he has been attending acting classes at HATTheatre. His writing skills include poems, song lyrics and scripts. He has performed his pieces on stages across Richmond, VA. He is a welcomed familiar face at Tuesday Verses and competitions held by The Writer's Den. His very first book of poetry, *Mixtape: The Book was released in 2017*. Other achievements include writing multiple short films, acting in films and performing in multiple stage productions. He currently lives in Henrico, VA.

Whether you liked this book, loved it or otherwise, thank you for giving it a chance.

-Ashton Lee

Where to follow Ashton Lee:

IG-@ashtonelijahlee
TokTok-@ashtonelijahlee

To contact for inquiries, my email is
ashtonleegd@gmail.com

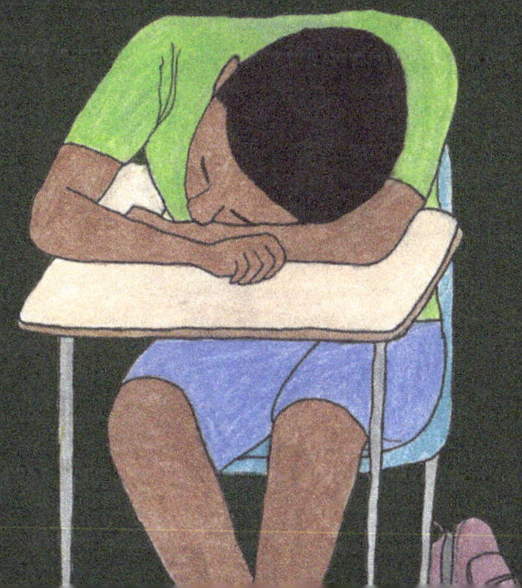

www.ingramcontent.com/pod-product-compliance
Lightning Source LLC
Chambersburg PA
CBHW061338120726
48001CB00002B/920